How To
START AND RUN
A
SUCCESSFUL
GRAPHIC
DESIGN
Studio

N A T   B U K A R

Printed in the United States of America

ISBN: 0-88108-092-6
Library of Congress Catalog Card Number: 91-072286

Second Printing, 1996

Published by
ART DIRECTION BOOK COMPANY
456 Glenbrook Road
Glenbrook, CT 06906
(203) 353-1441

ACKNOWLEDGEMENTS

My love and appreciation to my wife Elaine, and children Howard, Julie and Robert for their support and encouragement throughout this project.

And to son Howard in particular who, as editor and proofreader kept me on the right path.

I would also like to acknowledge the valuable suggestions made by:
    Mildred Sacks Zuckerman
    Martin Schneider
    Michael Neyer
and to:
    Joe Marcou, who enthusiastically gave of his time and the benefit of his experience in operating a successful package design studio.

TABLE OF CONTENTS

TABLE OF CONTENTS (cont.)

I started working in an ad agency art department the summer before my senior year in high school. Doing board work, assembling comps, mounting and cutting mats helped me get started when I graduated.

After years of doing board work, comping other designers' layouts and having most of my ideas and suggestions ignored, I went out on my own.

My ideas were good. I was a good solid designer. My strong point was my way of thinking, my ability to use graphics to communicate complex ideas.

I freelanced for some years, and in 1953 formed Presentation Designers in New York City with another designer, Kurt Larisch. We specialized in designing and producing sales and training presentations, which were then just coming into general use.

We introduced sophisticated graphics. We designed unusual formats. When slides started to take over the presentation business we introduced techniques already in use in animated films, dimensional characters, sculptural sets, and trick photography.

For example:

For Redbook Magazine we built a 6 foot tissue box. The pages popped up, were pulled out and hung on the wall.

We helped the Federal Reserve Bank explain its check processing system.

We assisted Junior Achievement in its 100th Anniversary celebration.

We explained to Union Carbide's truckers, of cryogenic gases, the safest procedures.

We told Redbook's, McCalls' and Family Circle's advertisers all about their magazines.

We helped the U.S. Navy train its pilots.

In the late sixties, another partner, David Sage, a talented film and promotion writer, joined us and we formed a Sales Promotion Company, and an Advertising Agency.

We have helped hundreds of companies sell their products and services, and in the process we learned how to operate a design business. And we did it in the toughest marketplace in the country, New York City.

We were burned, but we learned how to protect ourselves. We learned what worked, mainly by doing lots of things that didn't work.

When Kurt retired, and David left to concentrate on industrial film production, I operated the companies for a few more years and, in time, sold them.

I spent the next 15 years as an associate creative director, with an ad agency and as the creative consultant on a number of sound/slide and video film productions. Now retired, I work on a new art career... as a sculptor.

The information presented here is for those experienced graphic designers, package designers, art directors, illustrators, retouchers, photographers and board persons who want to go out on their own.

In the following chapters, I have provided all the information you need to get organized and operate in an efficient professional way. All the options are there. Just choose the ones you will be comfortable with.

As a police officer in the auto commercial says, relating the tale of a stolen auto, "You couldn't invent this stuff." The information here is distilled out of over 30 years of experience starting as a boardman, general free-lancer, then as an art director, associate creative director, and president of an advertising agency. And in addition, I was a founding partner in a well known A/V production house called Presentation Designers and a founding partner in a Sales Promotion Agency called Sage, Bukar & Larisch, Inc.

Starting out on your own is exciting. There's no one looking over your shoulder, telling you what to do and how to do it. There's no one to reject your best ideas. It's freedom! Independence! It's the opportunity to profit from your own ability.

It's doing the kind of work you always wanted to do. It's taking control of your life. Whether you achieve your highest goals, or succeed at a more modest level you will find your efforts rewarded by growth in confidence and self-esteem.

When everything goes well in a business, things tend to take care of themselves. However, when problems arise, knowing how to deal with them can make the difference between making or losing money. I have concentrated on these negative aspects of the business to provide the reader with fore knowledge of common problems they may encounter, the means to prevent their occurrence, and ways to deal with them when prevention is not possible.

1

Start with the Right Attitude

So you wanted to be an artist. It would be something you would enjoy doing. You could become an illustrator, or a graphic designer, or even a package designer.

You will be independent. Probably become rich and famous.

So you gather together your carefully assembled portfolio of school samples and go out to seek your future.

You get some experience, and work hard waiting for your talent to be discovered. But it doesn't happen and you don't know why. What are you doing wrong? What does it take to succeed?

You're talented, creative, intelligent, personable, confident and ambitious. That's what it takes and more.

Who will make it? Who won't!

I know artists with very ordinary design ability who are very successful in this business.

We all know people who are not artists, or creative, yet they run prosperous advertising companies, and design studios.

You know you're more talented than "what's-his-name." You're smarter than the senior art director. You say to yourself, "How come I don't have his job?" "Why are people with less talent and less brains getting ahead while I'm standing still?"

The answer may be that you are too much of an artist and not enough of a busineman!

It's easy to see how it can happen. You have spent years training yourself in all aspects of art and design. You have been taught to draw, to paint. You have been taught technique, and graphic design. You think, talk, and act like the artist that you are. You believe that design is everything. Your art becomes directly connected to your self-esteem. Your art becomes you.

Thus equipped, fine human beings that you are, you are thrown into this business of art. Where art is only a commodity, part of the process that makes money for everyone along the line from manufacturer to consumer. Unless you adapt to this marketing oriented world, success will pass you by. And in its place, as in the case of an artist I know, there rises an uncomprehending anger that builds up year after year until you hate and fight with everyone you have to work with.

In the advertising agencies, in the art studios that serve them, at the clients that support them there are many other jobs besides creative jobs. Non-art jobs like the financial controller, media buyer, marketing research, sales, computer operators, secretaries, and production people. They comprise the business people of your world. You will probably find about an eight to one ratio of them to creative people even at the advertising agencies.

The significance of this is not that creative talent isn't important. Creative talent is important. But the business or marketing aspects of the job are at least as important, and possibly even more important. Remember that the sharp business person can buy talent and succeed. The creative artist must become a business person to succeed. Sure, you could find a business oriented partner, But you will still need to produce and function within the requirements of the business world to succeed.

Talent is not enough. Only a graphic genius has the possibility of succeeding on creative ability alone. Genius is rare. The rest of us, talented as we all are, have to get to work on becoming better business people. While everybody else is occupied with business, making money for themselves, their employers or their clients, you probably have only been concerned with design and art.

If you are serious about design as a means to earn your livelihood, you have to understand and accept the idea that art, design, aesthetics are not the goal. They are only the means to the selling of ideas, the selling of products, and to the selling of services. Sales mean profits. Profits mean more money. That's what it is really all about.

If you are working in an advertising agency, or design studio you have been living in a totally different world from the world you are about to enter. It is the world of the entrepreneur, the world of business.

Up to now you have been surrounded by other artists, copywriters, and creative people with highly developed aesthetic values. Your work has been judged on the basis of how good your concepts were, how successfully your designs worked, and the appropriateness of your typeface selections.

The business people that you will now be dealing with make their judgments on other values.

Ask yourself this...how many of your friends, relatives, and neighbors who are not artists understand and appreciate the paintings and sculpture being done today?

Do you believe that the average vice president or any middle level manager in a large corporation, or even the top executives of smaller companies know any more about art, design, or aesthetics, than the people around you? Certainly, you will occasionally find an executive with a more knowledgeable eye, but most of your marketing people, promotion managers, or public relations people have no training and little interest in design. Their needs are expressed by their desire that it "looks nice" or "looks elegant", or it should "hit hard", or "be interesting looking." Some may have picked up a few "buzz" words but their aesthetic sense is only slightly more developed.

That is precisely why they need you. They trust you to do what they can not do. But you must use this creative ability, not only as an artist, but as a businessman as well. Evaluate your ideas in relation to the clients marketing needs. Question the client on the marketing aspects of the design project.

In most cases your efforts will be judged first, on how well they meet the marketing criteria, and if they hit the target, then by a personal aesthetic judgement.

The judgment they make that may kill the illustration you sweated over, is a business judgment. Will it help make money for me, or will I make more money if I change it, that is the thought process of the person passing judgment.

Understand that it is not that your designs are wrong. They're probably great. It's just that the client believes that the headline should be bigger to help his small space ad gain more attention in a large format newspaper. He believes that more attention, means more sales.

The pale green background tone you chose went perfectly with the dark blue lettering on the whiskey bottle label. But then the client says that green is a bad color for a whiskey product. It's an industry prejudice. What are you going to do? Fight it into the ground? Or, press your point of view, and when you feel he probably won't move, present your second choice color.

The client wants his company name, logo, address, and phone number to appear on every page of the catalog you have been asked to design. It creates an unexpected design challenge. . . and you thought this was an opportunity to design an award winner. Foiled again?

What the client knows is that his competitors, mostly smaller companies, xerox and use pages from his catalog as their catalog. Keeping his name and address on each page is his way of preventing them from doing this.

If you understand this basic fact, that you are involved like everyone else in a business, thinking in those terms will change many of the things that you are doing now that have been coming out wrong. Everything you now attempt to do has to reflect this new business/marketing perspective, as well as the artist's perspective.

Think like an artist, that is part of the business world. Know how to fit in. Create ideas that make marketing sense, as well as good graphic sense. Consider how what you do can make money for your clients. That's the basic question. Many of the answers will now come out somewhat differently. As a result, you will experience less disappointment, rather than more.

There are also negative aspects to this way of thinking. You will have to do things that you didn't want to do before. It may not have been "good design" to do them before, but now it may be "good business" to compromise.

I am not suggesting that you have no aesthetic responsibility. I believe that with an understanding of the proper role design has in the overall marketing picture, you can not only win awards for excellence in design, but win the clients accolades for executing a financially successful project as well.

With this new marketing oriented approach you will sell your work more easily. When you relate how the design works with the marketing concept, you will be talking to the clients in terms they understand. You will find that as you understand the sales and marketing strategies better, your designs and your ability to sell them will improve. The more your designs relate, the more readily they will be accepted. Less rejections. Less redo's. Less changes. More satisfied clients. More income for you.

2

Setting
Yourself Up
for Business

You've made the decision. You are going into business.

Now the first thing you need is a place to work, an office. An impressive address would be nice. Maybe a suite of offices. Carpeting. An attractive receptionist.

That certainly is an excellent way to go, but not many artists just starting out can afford that kind of investment.

Supporting an office and meeting the other expenses of doing business will be difficult unless you have a steady volume of work you can depend on.

It is a more practical approach to start with a minimum of expenses, until you have some idea of the volume of work you can expect to generate.

There are a number of ways to get started. Let's examine the options that are available to you.

1. Using your home or apartment as your office.

2. Work in exchange for space. (Bartering)

3. The independent in-house group.

4. Subleasing office space.

5. Sharing leased space.

6. Primary lease of space.

Let's look at the advantages and disadvantages of each approach.

1. The Home Office

If you live in a home or apartment that is attractively furnished, and located in an appropriate neighborhood, consider the possibility of using it as your first business office as well.

Is it large enough for you to set a room aside, or to use a suitable area within a room for your office?

Another consideration would be the length of your lease. If it is due for renewal, and not really suited for an office you might think about delaying the start of your business. You can start when you find another place more suitable. The home or apartments dual use as living quarters and business office may warrant some additional expenditure for an appropriate place. Starting your business at home and then moving it within a few months with the attending need to redistribute your new phone number to everyone you have called on, reprinting new stationary, and any promotional literature you distributed is not worth the effort.

The home/office would have to be conveniently located in terms of getting to and from your clients, and their ability to get to and from your office. The same would be true for suppliers, a photostat shop, or messengers, the services you need on a day by day basis to conduct your business. What about a nearby art supply store if you are caught short while working on a rush job? If you planned to install your own photostat processor, check whether the power needed is available.

The savings in additional rental expenses can make the inconvenience of a home office worthwhile. There also may be tax advantages to be considered. You may be able to deduct part of your rent as a business expense. This is also true of telephone, electricity, heating, and maintenance expenses. The Internal Revenue Service's list of allowable deductions changes from time to time. Check your accountant for specifics on what can and can not be deducted.

IRS for tax deductions

In addition to the economies of a home office there are other advantages as well. Jobs that require working long hours into the night are more readily handled working at home. There could also be significant savings of time otherwise spent commuting back and forth to an office. However, you might have to conduct more of your business meetings at your client's offices.

The convenience or inconvenience of the home office is very dependent on your personal situation. It would seem to be more suitable for a graphic designer or computer oriented designer, an illustrator or photo-retoucher, rather than for a photographer, for example.

The matter of a spouse, small children, noise, and other interferences such as visiting friends and relatives are considerations only you can evaluate. A large pet dog can be a problem. If it roams freely throughout the home, you can end up with a spilled bottle of ink on a just finished design.

While some artists are completely against a home office, others have successfully maintained this way of doing business for years.

2. Work in Exchange For Space

Work/space is a barter arrangement. For use of a company's space, you trade your services on some equitable basis.

This type of arrangement is common with advertising agencies and graphic design studios. They may have leased more space than they can use immediately to allow room for future expansion. They usually sub-lease or trade this space for services that are useful and convenient to have on their premises.

Illustrators, graphic designers, mechanical and assembly people, layout renderers, photographers and photo retouchers provide the kinds of services usually traded.

In this way the companies use unproductive space and have additional free-lance people available to help out when they get into periods of heavy activity.

In this type of arrangement you usually must give their work preference. This can lead to conflicts.

You may be working hard on a rush job for one of your own clients, and they come in with a job they need immediately. While there may come a time when you have no choice but to say no, most of the time some accommodation can be worked out. It may take some fancy footwork, late hours, and some smooth talking, but it usually works itself out.

Another problem with this kind of arrangement is that the agency or studio may have so much work on a continuous basis that it could limit your ability to get other business, and keep you from properly servicing your own clients.

If you are starting out without enough business to support yourself this may be a reasonable way to keep afloat until you build a base to operate completely independently.

If you really want to be able to build your business and remain independent, negotiate an agreement that trades a pre-determined number of hours for the space and specific services you are to receive, rather than an arrangement that gives you the space free.

One method of determining how to arrive at an equitable exchange of work for space, is to place a monetary value on the space and on the services you are to receive. Find out how much the going rate is per square foot of floor space in the area of the city where the office is located. The cost is usually quoted on an annual basis. Divide that figure by 12 and you have a monthly square foot figure to work from.

Multiply the width of the space under consideration by the depth of the space to determine the square footage.

Then multiply the square footage of the room by the cost per month of a sq. ft. and you have the monthly value of the space.

Add to this the value of any services being provided. Such as telephone installation, phone answering services, etc.

The sum arrived at is the total value of the space and services you are to receive.

Using your billing rate per hour you can now calculate how many hours a month you may need to exchange for the space and services.

Example:

The room or space is 9' x 10'. (90 sq. ft.)

The going rate for the space is $25. per sq. ft. annually.

```
        90.00 sq ft
    x $25.00 per sq ft
  $2250.00 annual cost
```

Divide $2250 by 12 for the monthly cost.

12/2250 = $187.50 per month

Add the monthly cost of a phone.

```
  $187.50
   150.00 phone
  $337.50 monthly total
```

If your hourly rate for the work you do is $35. per hour, divide $337.50 by 35. to find out how many hours you would have to work to pay for the space and phone.

35/337.50 = 9.64 hours

Then negotiate, by trading as few hours of work as you can for the space and services.

Whatever is agreed upon, put it in writing. It does not have to be a legal document drawn up by a lawyer. It can be as simple as a letter one of you writes to the other. It should spell out the broad terms that you both agreed upon. The purpose is for each of you to have a clear understanding of what has been agreed to. You can't depend upon a verbal agreement. People have bad memories. In verbal discussions, sometimes two people listening to the same thing understand it differently.

Whoever writes the letter should make two copies, one for each of you. Sign both copies and have the other party sign both copies as well. You should each keep a signed copy.

There are a few problems that generally come up during this type of arrangement and they should be settled right at the beginning.

Example:

If the company you have space with doesn't use up the alloted hours you owe them every month, what happens? Let's say that the company gets a quiet period and does not use you for three months. Does the time not used accumulate? Through no fault of your own you could end up owing the company a lot of time.

One answer is to agree to wipe the slate clean at the end of every month. If they do not use the time it is lost. It is their responsibility to use it or lose it.

What if the company needs twice as much of your time than was agreed upon? You should be paid for additional hours at an agreed upon hourly or per job rate.

Let me point out that these arrangements only work if they are equitable for both parties.

If, for example, the company only uses half their alloted time for a few months, and then uses twice as much the following month, it would be wise to consider the possibility of <u>not</u> billing for the extra time. This gesture would tend to equalize the advantages and not unbalance the relationship. If the relationship becomes unbalanced, more to the advantage of one party than to the other, resentment will develop and the arrangement will break-up.

The point is to cover yourself with an agreement, but don't necessarily hold to every word and comma. Bend when it makes sense to do so. Voluntarily adjust situations that may not be working out fairly. You can't be rigid in these situations.

An artist I knew had a good spot in an advertising agency that provided him with free space, phone service and lots of billable hours every week. One day he was called in by the production manager who explained that they had badly under-estimated a job he had worked on. They said that they were asking everyone that worked on the job to reduce their charges somewhat. They explained that they would still lose money on the job, but that this way their loss would be minimized. This artist believed in the principal that he had to be paid for every hour that he worked, and refused to cooperate.

Within a few weeks he was called in and told that his space was needed, and he would have to leave. If this bill cutting was a common practice of the agency he would have been justified in his refusal to reduce the invoice. However this was an unusual occurrence, it had only happened once before in the year and six months he had been there. He was profiting from the arrangement with the agency, and when he was asked to give a little, he refused. He allowed the situation to become unbalanced in his favor, and this was not acceptable. Not a smart business decision. He lost a lot more than he would have had he cooperated.

One of the hard lessons to learn is that in business it isn't necessary to be right, just to <u>win</u>.

This artist, in insisting that he be paid in full for his labors, was justified according to his principals, but he lost a pretty good deal that probably would have lasted a lot longer than it did.

3. The Independent In-house group

A company that has an uneven flow of graphic work, very busy periods alternating with long slow periods, may sometimes be interested in eliminating expensive salaried employees. They may try using only free-lancers. But that usually doesn't work out on a long time basis. You may occasionally see an ad placed by an advertising or promotion agency in local newspapers or trade papers, suggesting this kind of arrangement, but generally it develops between an agency and the artists working with them.

A company experiencing this problem for some time may approach an employee, or a free-lancer they are using a great deal of the time, and suggest that they take over the art department. The usual idea is that they will give all their work to this new company. And that this company will occupy the space that was their art dept.

These circumstances lead to an opportunity for ambitious artists to start their own business.

There is no reason why an artist who knows that an agency is having this kind of erratic work flow problem can't initiate the subject, and suggest this as a possible solution himself rather than wait to be approached by the agency.

What this arrangement does for the artist starting this way, is provide him with the knowledge that a certain amount of work will be coming in. It provides a base upon which to build a business. It also solves the office problem at the same time. A rent payback arrangement is usually part of the deal. Follow the procedure outlined in the preceding work/space section to determine the value of the space and services being provided. In this case since you are to take over an existing art department there may also be included charges for the equipment and furnishings that come with the offices.

One problem with this type of arrangement is that if there is a strong flow of work, it will be

difficult to arrange time to build additional business on the outside. It takes a great deal of
discipline to make the time to solicit new business. Unless you can build your own independent business, you are just a satellite of the company, practically an employee. There is also a
danger that if the flow of work stays heavy the
company may want to revert back to full time
employees, and terminate your arrangement. If
you have developed outside business you can
move and continue doing business. If you have-
n't and are dependent on the agency for most of
your business, you will be out of business.

This arrangement also requires that you be pro-
tected by a written agreement. One that covers
the length of time the arrangement is to be in
effect, terms covering renewal of the agreement
and for dissolving the agreement as well. It
should also cover the rental agreed upon and the
services to be provided. It should describe what
kinds of design and production services it is
obligated to purchase from your company, and
what services it can purchase elsewhere. This
kind of arrangement is too complex for a mere
exchange of letters. You should protect your
interests by having an attorney look over the
agreement before you sign it.

4. Sub-lease Space From a Larger Company

To sub-lease commercial office space, you must
find a company that has extra space it no longer
needs. The company may have leased extra space
for future expansion. A company in the process
of reorganization may want to realize some revenue from the space it no longer needs. This is

preferred to the alternative of moving which can be very expensive.

In large urban business centers, this is generally the only way to obtain small, one to three room office units. Real estate brokers are generally not interested since the commissions would be small.

These smaller office units can be found by "putting out the word" to everybody you know that is in a position to hear of available office space. Canvass the areas that you are interested in. Talk to building superintendents, elevator operators, or security personnel. Check the classified real estate ads in your newspapers. Watch for ads in the business trade press, as well as advertising, and other art publications. If all else fails, you can run your own ad in the trade press or local newspapers describing what you are looking for.

Before you make a decision on which office is the best one for your needs, here are some things that you may want to consider:

Commuting. Choose a location that is convenient to get to from your home. You do not want to spend hours going to and from your place of business. Is the office near a superhighway with an exit nearby? Is it convenient to public transportation? Does it have enough parking facilities? Is there a good choice of restaurants available nearby? What about an art supply store? Will you have access to art supplies on an emergency basis?

Access. Direct access from the elevator or from the entrance hall to your office space is most desirable, but not always possible in a sublease.

In many cases entry would be first into the reception area of the prime tenant, and then through their offices to your offices. If you can have direct access from their reception area, that is also a good arrangement.

If you can not share the reception area and the receptionist with the company leasing space to you, establish a reception space of your own within your space at the entry area.

Even if you can't afford a receptionist at the start, you don't want your office visible to anyone that comes through your entry door.

Urban Business Center. Every city will have its prestigious business center. This will be the most expensive office space in town. There can usually be found around the edges of this prime area, well maintained older buildings that will be considerably less expensive and still be very presentable. Check the public areas of the building. See if the lobby and halls are clean and properly maintained. If possible walk into one of the tenants in the building, and ask if there is anything that they are unhappy about concerning the building.

Residential. In many small towns, rural or suburban areas, there are large homes that have been converted to office use. There are also small city apartments, and older one family brownstones that have been converted to office use. These are generally less expensive than regular business office space, and generally work out very well.

Loft/Manufacturing space. Loft space, imaginatively converted and decorated makes for an "arty" unconventional atmosphere that could be advantageous to a graphic design company, advertising or sales promotion agency, or package designer.

5. Sharing Leased Space

The opportunity to share leased space can occur when two groups in similar but non-competitive businesses decide to lease a space and share common areas. It would work with any combination of ad agency, graphic art service, industrial film producer, printing broker, package designer, or photographer. Each company on its own may not be able to afford to establish an impressive office, but together, two companies can share a reception area, a receptionist, conference room, storage areas and maintenance services. In this way both establish a larger, more impressive office, without the costly duplication of facilities that are not used by either company on a full time basis.

The type of space that works best for this kind of arrangement is space that can be separated into two groups of offices, each of which has an entrance from a common reception area.

Decide which company has responsibility for the shared facilities, or you may find yourself, as I did, in a situation where the shared receptionist was not being supervised by anyone. Weeks after the receptionist was hired we learned that she was calling our messenger service each day, at $10.50 a trip, to pick up her lunch at a restaurant she preferred across town. She was asked to find another job, closer to her favorite restaurant.

It is also a good idea to have the receptionist log appointments for use of the common areas, (conference room, projection room) in advance to work out conflicting schedules and avoid problems.

This is an arrangement that works well where all the parties are reasonable, and able to talk out conflicts in a calm understanding manner. It's for friends, or people you can get along with very well. It is not something you would want to do with strangers. It worked so well for us that we even organized an after hours life drawing class that people from both companies attended.

This is not an arrangement meant for the long term. Don't sign a long term lease unless you write in a provision that one or the other of the two companies can, upon agreement, take over the entire space.

What generally happens in this arrangement is that one or both companies grow and require additional space. The obvious solution is that one company stays and the other moves to other quarters. Or they may both want to move to separate larger quarters.

When it comes to signing a lease the landlord may want to lease to only one company rather than to both companies. If that is the case, write an agreement between yourselves that both of your companies share the responsibility of the leased space. Then one company can sign the lease, and the other can sign the agreement at the same time. Your lawyers should be advised of what you are contemplating. You and your lawyer should carefully check the lease before it

25

is signed. <u>Do not leave it all to your lawyer</u>. He knows generally what is good for you and what would be bad for you, but only you have the intimate knowledge of your business requirements, so read it carefully even when the lawyer has approved it, before you sign it.

6. Direct Lease of Space

This means leasing a suitable office for your new company exclusively. There is no sharing, unless you want to sublease some space to lessen your overhead expenses. This is a step to be taken only when you have a steady flow of work coming in, and cash reserves to cover your expenses for a period of at least six months.

The same considerations given to the selection of sub-leased office space would also apply here: location, transportation, size, cost, etc.

When you are presented with a form lease to sign, have an experienced real estate lawyer check it out for you, then check it carefully yourself.

The lease provisions as presented by the landlord or his broker does not have to be accepted as is. The landlord will make the lease as advantageous to himself as he possibly can. You can request whatever changes you want. The final version of the lease will probably contain some of the changes you requested and a number of clauses that the landlord would not remove from the document.

Other Important Considerations

Security can not be ignored. In large cities it is a big problem. Receptionists lose their purses, and others lose their wallets, when they are taken out of hanging jackets and coats by thieves who are allowed to enter and roam freely among the offices. What kind of security does the building provide? Are windows and doors well secured? Is there a doorman or elevator starter in the lobby? Is there an alarm system for each floor or each office? Is access to the elevators restricted?

Fire & Smoke Alarms. Is the building provided with proper fire prevention; alarms, fire extinguishers? Are fire escape routes laid out on every floor? Are fire exits clear and accessible? Is there a sprinkler system?

Windows. The more there are the better. Artists need light, and something to look at while their thinking up their next great design. Some artists just can not work in a space without windows. To others it doesn't seem to matter.

Lighting. Check for sufficient ceiling and ambient light.

Electric Power. Are there enough electrical outlets convenient to the drawing boards for table lamps, pencil sharpeners, light tables? Is there sufficient power to run computers, photostat machines, projection equipment?

Air-conditioning. Who has responsibility for maintenance? Are there ducts in every room? Is it included in the rent?

Heating. What kind of heat is provided? Who is

responsible for maintenance? Is it included in the rent?

Access. Is the building open seven days a week? Is it open on holidays? Can you get in when the building is closed? Is it accessible 24 hours a day? If the building closes early, can you stay as late as necessary?

Lease. How long a lease is offered? How long a lease are you interested in? A long lease protects you from increases while you are growing. A short lease means fewer obligations if things don't work out.

Painting. Does the space require painting? Or repairs? Who is responsible for getting it done?

Cleaning & Maintenance. Will daily cleaning and waste removal be included? Will window cleaning and floor waxing be provided? How often? Will the windows be washed? How often?

3

How to Price Your Work

The two factors that will most influence your chances for success as a business are your commitment to go out and get the work, and your ability to produce it satisfactorily. You have already proven your ability to produce, you have worked in the field for some time, gained experience and now you're going out on your own. Now, you have to find the work before you can do it. One of the many things that will influence your ability to get the work is how you price yourself.

Naturally, if you price yourself high, you limit your available market to those few who want the best and can afford to pay top dollar for it. Unless you have already built a reputation as a top designer, your volume will be small and the going will be rough. If you price yourself too low, you probably will find that you're doing a lot of business but the profits at the end of the year may not make it all worthwhile.

The idea is to find the proper pricing level that will give you the income you want, while staying competitive with others of equal experience and ability.

To establish a pricing structure, a minimum hourly rate must be established. This rate is calculated to cover all estimated expenses and your minimum salary requirements. This minimum hourly figure is not used to estimate a job, but it is the starting point, a base line, to which we add when estimating a job.

To determine your basic hourly rate, add together all of your fixed expenses:

	cost per month
Rent and maintenance	$ 600.
Minimum salary required	3400.
Telephone	200.
General office supplies; stationary, postage, etc.	100.
Accounting & legal services	250.
Advertising & Promotion	250.
	Total $4800.

Let's say that the total is $4800. a month. You will have to pay these expenses (except salary) regardless of how much or how little business you do.

Now figure out how many billable hours you have available every month. Even if you work a 40 hour week, (160 hours a month) you probably will not have more than 80-85 billable hours per month.

Some of your time will be spent soliciting business. Some time will be lost to record-keeping and billing. More time will be lost estimating projects you do not get.

Now take the monthly expense total $4800. and divide it by the amount of billable hours (85) and the result is $56. per hour.

$56. is your minimum hourly rate.

If that was the rate you actually charged, you would just break even. That is, you would recover your expenses and meet your minimum salary requirements. But you will have made no profit.

No profit also means no funds for future expansion.

If you're starting with only a small nest egg, enough to cover up to three months of operating expenses, without any profits coming in, you will soon be dependent on your cash receivables. One large project can keep you busy for three months, and use up all your cash, your working capital. You're broke until the checks start coming in. That probably won't start until 30, 60, or 90 days after the job is billed. How do you stay alive while you're working? Accumulated profits left in the business, that's how!

Your minimum figure should be below what is generally being charged. How does it compare to the rates being charged by other competitive firms doing business in your area? Check with your contacts in the business, friends, classmates, people you've worked with.

You have decided that you want to make a profit of 25%.

Example:

$56.15 minimum hourly rate
x 25% profit

25 x 56.15 = 14.04

56.15 minimum rate
14.04 profit
70.19 hourly rate

Should you find that your minimum rate plus your profit is below the going rates in your area its easy to adjust it upwards. If the rate you calculated is too high, it means that your fixed expenses are too high, for the type of work you are going after. If the fixed expenses can not be reduced, then you probably have set an unrealistic earnings goal, and must reduce it to stay competitive.

If your competition has a setup that is similar to yours and is charging less, their earning expectations are probably lower than yours. If that isn't the case, you can be sure they won't be around for long. After checking the rates around town you will have an idea of what the top and bottom rates are. Knowing how you compare in terms of creativity, service, and experience to the competing companies will give you an idea of how much to raise your minimum rate.

Now with the knowledge of your minimum rate and your competitive rate, you have a basis on which to start estimating.

ESTIMATING

There are a number of factors that go into estimating the cost of a job:

     First: <u>how long you think the job is going to take to do</u>. You can only estimate the time accurately after you have questioned the client on all aspects of the work. Does he want to see roughs first, or comprehensive layouts before proceeding into finished art. Does the client want to see pencils before an illustration is

34

completed. How many times do you have to go back for OK's? Are you going to get involved in a lot of meetings that eat up lots of time?

Until you have a clear understanding of what is wanted, you cannot accurately estimate any job.

Second: in addition to figuring out your time/cost on a job, there are a number of products and services you may have to provide to complete an assignment. Whatever purchases are to be made, must also be considered when estimating. You are entitled to a reasonable mark-up on things like typesetting, photostats, printing, and photography.

You may also need to hire freelancers to help out on a job, or sub-contract part of the job to an illustrator, or photo-retoucher. These costs must also be considered in your estimate, and marked-up to provide you with additional profits.

This chart will give you some idea of the amounts generally added to the cost of these products and services by advertising agencies, studios, and freelancers.

	Percent Mark-up
Photography	50-100
Photostat	20-40
Printing	
small jobs up to $25,000	20-40
over $25,000	20-25
Freelancers	50-100
Illustration	50-100
Typesetting	20-40

Third: you also need to consider how the work is to be used. If it is to appear in a major publication, you should charge more than if it is going into an inexpensive trade publication. A promotion piece to be used just once, should be less than a manual that will be used for years.

Fourth: consider who the client is. If the buyer is the end user, and there are no intermediaries you can charge top dollar. If you were doing it for their advertising agency, you would have to charge less, to leave room for the agency's mark-up. If the assignment is coming from a studio that is doing it for the advertising agency, then you may have to charge even less to leave room for their mark-up as well. As a free-lancer that might be OK. But, the price could be below your minimum and then you can't afford to take the assignment.

You can see that you can't charge the same price regardless of the number of hands the job passes through. Then again, you have to get at least your minimum, plus some profit, however small, and not worry about the job becoming too expensive and being cancelled. If you work below your minimum you are actually working for nothing. You will not earn enough to meet your expenses or provide a minimum salary.

Fifth: consider what rights you are assigning to the purchaser? They could have the right to reproduce it one time or many times. The purchaser may want to purchase all rights to the work. The more rights you assign to the purchaser, the more the cost should be for the work. You can sell the original or retain the original, even if you assign the buyer reproduction rights.

ESTIMATING ON-THE-SPOT

One day shortly after you have started your business a client will call up and say to you "John, I have a layout job I need done right away." "It's a color brochure and I need it back by Thursday." "Can you come right over?" You go to his office and after explaining the job to you, he asks, "Can you give me an estimate of what it will cost right now?"

<u>Avoid doing it!</u> Do not give him an estimate unless you are absolutely sure that you have all the information and you have considered all the factors. Don't be pushed into a quick cost estimate on the spot, there's too much of a chance that you will forget something, and you could end up losing money on the job.

Assure the client that you will get back to him within the hour, then do your estimating carefully when you get back to your office. If your client is insistent, and you see that he really needs the cost estimate immediately, and you must quote on the spot, carefully calculate the price and then add an additional ten or fifteen percent to cover anything that you may have forgotten. Use an estimating form that has all the cost categories listed. That's the best way to be sure you haven't forgotten an item. If you follow this procedure, you will spend a lot less time regretting your quick low estimates.

There are art buyers who use this technique, of asking for an estimate on the spot, to trap the unwary, especially if they are telling you that they don't have much money for this job.

Just take it easy. Pricing, like anything else important has to be carefully considered. Under pressure, an artist might only consider how many hours a job will take, without allowing a safety margin, and not considering the other factors we have discussed.

An estimate should mean that the price is approximate, but that is not the case here. In this business, an estimate really is not an estimate, it is in reality a bid. Whatever amount you quote is all you will be allowed to charge, unless the specifications change.

If you do provide an estimate, either on the spot, or over the phone, ask the client to send you his purchase order. If you do not receive it before you are to start work on the project, send the client two copies of your estimate, both signed by you. Include the price agreed upon, delivery date, the terms of payment, the reproduction rights that are assigned the purchaser, and a description of the job, quantity, number of pages, how many colors etc. Request that he sign one copy and return it to you.

In that way your estimate becomes confirmed by the client, and functions in place of a purchase order.

Let us examine what could happen next. You have been assigned a job at an agreed upon price. As you begin working on it, the client makes changes which alter the dimensions of the job. He may change an eight page assignment into a 12 page assignment, or change from two colors to three. Whatever changes the client makes that add work to the job must be dealt with <u>immedi-</u>

ately. Before you do anything make certain that the client understands that there will be additional charges, and provide a revised estimate in writing as soon as possible.

When he sees the additional cost, he will either say OK and revise your purchase order or change his mind and cancel the changes.

If you do not settle it before hand, you may be left holding the bag at the end. Especially when the client denies that the changes were important enough to warrant added charges.

It happened to me on a big job with a large respected corporation, and I lost $10,000. worth of additions, when they wouldn't come up with any additional money to cover extensive changes they made.

There is another technique that can be used with difficult small accounts that are always complaining about the high cost of your services.

These bargain hunters think every estimate is too high. Their budgets somehow are never large enough to meet your prices. These people only feel comfortable when they can get you to reduce your price. They must buy it for less.

Knowing your minimum rate will give you a basis for refusing to take jobs that have a budget below that rate, since you know that you will lose money if you do take those jobs.

On your first meeting with this type of buyer, and assuming that you have asked all the right questions, you should quote a competitive price that is based on your regular rates. If you find that the client does not have the budget to meet your price, find out how much is available for the job. If you can meet his budget price and stay above your minimum rate, you probably would want to consider reducing your price to the client's available funds, and take the job.

The next time this client calls for an estimate, you must protect yourself by assuming that the same thing will happen again. Add ten or fifteen percent to your normal price when you quote. If you are again asked to reduce your estimate, you can do so (after resisting their efforts) to your normal price and you will make the profit you are entitled to. If you raise your normal price and the client does not try to reduce it, you are just that much better off. You have also learned that this client may not be a bargain-hunter, and also, that he can be charged at a higher rate.

Your pricing must be balanced. It must stay flexible, competitive, and must bring you a profit on every job if you are to succeed. Without profits to build up your bank account, you will always be dependent on cash flow, the checks that come in, to pay your immediate expenses.

Organizing
a Sales Portfolio

Samples of your work, both original and reproductions, are at the heart of your ability to demonstrate what you can do. Therefore it is necessary to set up a filing system to retain samples of your work as they are produced.

Attempts should be made to get back particularly good design and layout originals after they have been reproduced. Requesting copies of printed pieces and ads you have created must be a constant occupation to keep your portfolio current. Try to obtain more than one copy of these samples, since you will need to replace them to keep your portfolio looking clean and neat.

Graphic designers and package designers working on projects that go through a number of stages of development, (logos, letterheads, new product packaging) should shoot slides of all the development designs as well as the final product. This documentation provides case histories for use as part of the portfolio.

The arrangement of your sample files will depend upon the requirements of your particular specialty.

The categories should relate to the way prospective buyers view samples of your work. If you are an illustrator, and a prospective buyer needs an illustration of a woman working at a kitchen sink, he will want to see what you have done on that particular subject.

If you are a package designer, and a client is

looking for a new cosmetic package, he will want to see what you have done for cosmetics. He does not want to see your best frozen food package.

It would make sense, then, to organize your sample files as follows:

Cosmetics

Frozen Foods

Drugs and Toiletries

Toys

Graphic Designers might file samples this way:

Annual Reports

Corporate Identity Programs

Sales Promotion

Direct Mail

Illustrators could file samples as follows:

Figures

Technical Subjects

Still Life

Children

METHODS OF PRESENTATION

Again, your specialty, and the type of clients that you are soliciting will determine the best method of presentation for your purpose.

1. Color Slides (35mm)

While color slides can be used by any artist, they make the most sense for the package designer, display or point of purchase designers, and the audio-visual designer. For these artists, actual samples would be too bulky to carry around from prospect to prospect. It requires that you carry the projection equipment, or arrange with your prospect to have projection equipment available for your meeting. If you are not representing one of these specialties, it probably would be more convenient to carry actual samples.

You could use a synchronized soundtrack with the slides to make a very professional presentation. You would need to carry an additional cassette recorder, or one of the slide projector units that incorporate slides and sound into a single unit. If you go this route, you may find it more convenient to use videotape instead.

2. Video Tape (Beta, VHS, 8mm)

Video cassettes are a natural way for art directors, industrial film producers, and slide-film producers to show what they have done to prospective clients. Films can easily be converted to video cassettes. Video cassettes are easier to view. Play back equipment is more readily available.

Today, there is a video player of some kind in every conference room. Inform your prospects of your equipment needs so that they can arrange to have what you need available for your meeting.

3. Portfolio

The art portfolio is still the most commonly used method of presentation for graphic designers, and art directors working mostly in print. It can be as simple as the big red envelope tied with a string (which I do not recommend). Or, as elaborate as a custom-made leather covered case. The portfolios most commonly used are the three-ring, or multi-ring binders, with acetate sleeves to hold the samples. Another popular form is the leatherette covered box with self-contained easel. This box can hold separate cards which are taken from the front and stored in the back as the presentation is made. In another version it contains a ring binder across the top, and the pages are flipped over and stored in the back during presentation.

Many artists like to have their flat print samples laminated to protect them. A flannel-like material is put on the back so that they do not scratch each other when they are stacked in a box. This is also an attractive way to present samples.

The physical part of your portfolio presentation, the case you carry it in, is important. The more professional the entire package looks the better first impression you will make. The artist that walks in with a shabby torn manila envelope will not receive the same reception that an artist with a custom made leather case will get. I'm not suggesting that every artist buy a fancy leather case, but the carrying case should be given careful consideration. The package should not only look good, it must protect the contents against the elements. It should also be suitable for the organization and presentation of your specific samples. It should be constructed so that changes in the materials can be made quickly and conveniently.

What you choose to show and how you present yourself will have a direct bearing on how successful you are. Your samples are not only a reflection of your talent, training, and experience, but of your personality as well. It tells the viewer whether you are logical and orderly, or not. That you are careful or careless.

Your portfolio is your salesman. In many cases you will not have seen the buyer before. In some cases your portfolio is all the buyer will see, since sometimes you will be asked to leave your portfolio with the receptionist. Your first impression will be made by your portfolio.

Artists proud of their work sometimes fill their portfolios with everything they have ever done. That is not the way to build a good selling portfolio.

The portfolio is your sample case, your work display. If you show good line illustration, you will get line illustration assignments. If you show great figure illustration, that's the kind of work assignments you will get. But, if the customer is looking for machine illustrations, and you show figure illustrations you will not get the assignment. You can insist to the buyer that you do great machine illustrations, but, if you do not show the kind of samples that they are looking for, you will never sell the buyer, even if you really can do great machine drawings.

Experienced buyers can tell whether your style or design ability is what they are looking for after seeing the first five samples. That's true no matter what you are selling. Therefore I believe that you should put your best samples first. Many artists don't agree with me. There are as many opinions on how to arrange your samples, as there are artists. Try different ways. Experiment! When you notice that one particular arrangement gets more response, stay with it. You have found what works for you. Since nothing is perfect, or permanent, keep experimenting. Try to keep perfecting your portfolio and presentation techniques. Never stop! Times change. Styles, attitudes, fads, all keep things constantly in motion. Keep pace with your times.

My approach was to try to make a good first impression. My best samples were followed by samples that had a direct bearing on the needs of the particular prospect I was calling on. At the end I added a few pieces to round out the picture.

You don't always get to go through your entire presentation. The prospect may be very pressed for time. They will flip through the first few pages, and then say that they have seen enough to know what you can do. They probably can, too. While it isn't a pleasant way to be treated it does happen once in a while. Most buyers if they make appointments will give you the ten or twenty minutes you need to tell your story. Try not to take more than twenty minutes.

Position only one piece of work on a page, unless the samples are very small and they all relate to a single campaign.

The more organized the materials are the better impression you will make.

If you are a designer, show your rough layouts, and the comp layout that led up to the printed piece being shown. The client is interested in seeing the whole working process. It isn't necessary to do it for everything in the portfolio; two or three examples should be enough.

Occasionally you will not have samples even close to the subject or style that is requested. In that case find anything that can be related. If a buyer needs a full color illustration of a plane in a stormy sky, and the closest sample you have is a cow in a green pasture with a stormy sky, or an illustration of a warship on a stormy sea, show them, and talk it the rest of the way. You may or may not get the assignment, but you are doing the best that you can under the circumstances.

Another thing to remember is that your samples, once chosen should not be set in concrete, never changed. A portfolio should be flexible, it should be changeable, so that it can be individualized for each sales call. Let's say that a client has to assign a layout for a cosmetic product catalog. He calls in three designers. They all show equally competent design abilities. One shows a drug and toiletries catalog he designed last year. Another shows a beautiful gift-ware catalog just completed. The third designer shows some great fashion ads from the major magazines.

The designer showing the drug and toiletries catalog would probably get the assignment, everything else being equal. He has shown a similar project done well. The buyer hasn't seen a cosmetic catalog, but it is close enough for him to be comfortable with the designer's ability to do it well. While the other two designers have shown the talent needed for the job, the fact that they had not previously done a cosmetic products catalog does not allow the buyer to feel secure enough to give them the job. This buyer attitude requires that we keep a sample file from which can be selected the kind of work needed for any type of sales call.

I think it is essential to talk along with the samples as they are shown. Every sample has a reason for being there. Tell why, let the prospect know that you can think as well as design. Don't talk about every piece in the portfolio. Choose three or four of the best examples and explain the problem and solution each represents.

If you are going after a narrow specialty, like figure illustration, leave your furniture illustration out. But, keep them on file ready to whip out when the need for a furniture illustration arises.

If you are showing package designs, show the finished packages, but include the selected comp layout and some of the preliminary designs to show the complete process. Include background materials that set up the marketing objectives. Present materials that relate your designs to the competitive environment.

No matter what you are selling: illustrations, advertising, annual reports, promotion, don't show only finished work. Show tissues, comps and roughs as well. After all, anybody can pick up printed pieces and claim that they designed them.

5

Prospecting
for
New Business

Your first efforts at getting new business would naturally be to contact just about everybody you know in and out of the business: classmates, former employers, friends, relatives, neighbors.

This certainly is a good way to get started. But you will find it difficult to build a successful business that lasts this way.

Then how do you get additional new business?

To build a real business, you must become a salesman. Contrary to what some artists believe, artists make good salesmen. Especially when they have to sell themselves. Selling is nothing more than convincing the buyer that you know how to solve his problem. You do this, in its simplest terms, by convincing him that you have the experience, and the creativity to do the job. Also, that you are dependable and easy to work with, and that your work is competitively priced.

First select a business or industry that you have some experience working with. You probably gained some insight into a number of different kinds of companies in the studios or advertising agencies you have worked for before going out on your own.

There are two basic ways in which you can prospect for new business:

Warm canvassing

Warm canvassing consists in finding potential

clients who indicate that they may be interested in your services. These potentially interested prospects can be found by a number of methods.

> **A) Sales letters** mailed to a list of companies within a particular industry. These letters can include a response card. Each response card returned is followed up by a phone call to set or confirm an appointment.

> **B) Advertising or sales promotion** mailings that enable the receiver to respond through the use of a coupon, a return postcard, or a phone call.

This is the preferred method of selling. You are making a personal call on a prospect who is interested. He will let you try to convince him to buy your services. It is much easier than cold canvassing.

Cold Canvassing

Cold canvassing means contacting prospects who do not know you. You have no way of knowing if they need your services. However you can increase the odds in your favor by selecting industries that you know use the services you are selling.

Cold selling is generally done by phone. Few artists like doing it, but if you master it's techniques you <u>will</u> build your business.

Some artists are cowed by the important titles of the people they are calling. The trick is to think of the person on the other end of the phone as an ordinary human being like yourself, which they are, somebody who would smile at a joke, who appreciates what you are trying to do. They know you are not calling to annoy them, but that you are calling to tell them about your services, which they may very well need. Most of the time you will find that they want to be helpful. If they can't use your services, they may direct you to the proper person in the company.

Learn how to have fun while selling by phone. If you need help in developing a good phone technique check your local public libraries, or book stores. A number of good books have been written on the subject of telemarketing or selling by phone. The local phone company business office is a good place to start. They may have free brochures available.

Building Personal Contacts

Make it your business to take every opportunity to meet people in the business. Attend trade shows, introduce yourself to suppliers, and hand out business cards to everyone. If appropriate, participate in seminars and workshops. Talk to the other participants, introduce yourself to the speakers. Take every opportunity that presents itself to "network," to meet and talk to people who may either be potential clients themselves, or have the connections to introduce you to potential prospects. When an opportunity arises, participate as a speaker at a seminar or trade show. Select a subject you know. A new or different facet of a subject that can be promoted. It will bring you attention, and business opportunities.

If possible, and in a subtle way, speak up at social functions. You may be with someone who is looking for your expertise right at that moment.

Public Relations, Advertising, & Sales Promotion

Public Relations is the method to use to promote yourself when you're starting out. It is the least expensive method of making yourself known to the business community. As a new business you have news value, with the trade press, and local newspapers.

Prepare a mailing list of the business editors of all the newspapers, magazines, and trade papers appropriate to your specialty. Write a news release stating that on such and such a date, the Smith Company was formed at this address, to perform the following services. Make it sound as interesting as you can. Duplicate it, enclose a photo of yourself if you like, and mail it out to your list. If you have the time, you can increase your chances of getting your release into print by following up with phone calls to the editors. If you can come up with an interesting story angle, you may develop the item into an article about yourself and your new enterprise.

Anytime you move your office, get an important new account, or add a new person to your staff; you have another opportunity to get your name into the papers.

Whenever you come up with a new solution to an old problem, or do anything new or innovative, you have an opportunity for an article in the trade press.

Advertising is a good way to build business, but it is expensive. It doesn't work well unless you are consistent, running ads over long periods of time.

Choosing the best vehicle for your campaign is difficult. Business newspapers are good but very broad based. It's the "shotgun" approach. You are paying to reach a lot of people who are not potential customers. If you are seeking clients in certain specialized industries placing ads or publicity in their trade journals would be more economical.

Advertising in the yellow pages of your local phone directory may be one way to get started.

Sales Promotion, an elaborate brochure showing your work, or a simple letter sent out to a specific list of companies gets you the best value for your dollar. That is, if you get the right mailing list.

A brochure is valuable as a "leave behind", when you make a sales call, or it can be mailed to a prospect you have seen and not heard from for a few months.

Another form of sales promotion is to enter industry competitions. Awards and display of your work all help to get you publicity and build your reputation. Clients love to see their projects winning awards. Be sure to give a framed copy of any awards won to the client.

No matter which method you choose to get business, you will have to determine the following:

Who do you want to contact? What business group or industry do you want to concentrate on?

Are you interested in small or large companies, or doesn't it matter?

Who is the best person to contact (job title,) at the companies you have chosen to contact ?

Start at the top. If it's a small company, contact the president. He will speak to you himself, or direct you to lower level management. In many cases it's the president that handles, promotion, advertising, etc.

In large companies, start with the highest possible title. For example, if you are selling promotion concepts, call the director of marketing rather than the advertising or sales promotion managers. If they don't want to talk to you, they will direct you to the proper lower level.

If you don't know who to contact in a particular company, the receptionist will guide you to the right person. In a large company, you can get that kind of information from the personnel manager.

When you have determined the industries you want to go after, the type of companies within those industries, and the job titles to contact, you will need to compile a list of these prospects.

The information you will need is:

❑ company name
❑ address

❏ phone number

❏ names and titles of personnel

You will also want to keep a continuing record of what happens as you pursue each prospect.

The system that many people use is a 3" x 5" card file. A card is made for each company to be contacted. One side of the card lists:

> company name
>
> address
>
> phone number

and notes on what happened when they were contacted.

Here is an example:

```
┌─────────────────────────────────────────────┐
│                                             │
│  John Smith Corporation      718-111-00000  │
│  1234 Main Street                           │
│  New York NY 11300                          │
│                                             │
│  4/12/89 Called T.M., out of town, be back Thur. │
│  Apptmt T.M. 4/19. Showed samples, will try me   │
│  as soon as the right assignment comes along.    │
│  Keep in contact.                           │
│                                             │
└─────────────────────────────────────────────┘
```

The entire back of the card is used to maintain the constantly changing names, titles, and the direct dial phone numbers of the people to be contacted.

When a company is located in an unfamiliar area, it's a good idea to enter travel directions on the card.

There are numerous ways to arrange the cards in

a file. You will, in a very short time determine the system that works best for you.

Here are some suggestions to get you started:

Create a section for the new companies that you are going to call.

Start another section for companies that you have called on. These cards need to be gone through periodically. The companies that have shown interest, but have not called in 1-3 months, should be called again.

Another section can be for companies with whom you have pending future appointments. These appointments should also be noted in an appointment book.

Some companies may ask to be called back in the future. "Call us back in six months, when we start planning our next promotion." Or, "Call us next year, we have spent our budget for the current year." You do not want to forget about them, so divide a section of your card file into the months of the year and file these cards there.

After a time you will have a number of company cards that you know have little or no possibility of turning into clients. Instead of throwing them out keep them in a separate "dead" section. The reason for keeping them is to check new lists against them. You don't want to waste your time re-calling these dead companies.

How to Compile a Prospect List

Prospect lists can be culled from a number of publications that list the information you need.

The "Yellow Pages" of the phone company will list companies by the products or services that they provide.

The Standard Directory of Advertisers will provide the names of companies that advertise, and the names, and titles of the personnel involved. In addition it provides information on number of employees, sales volume in dollars, and the names of products or services provided.

Standard & Poor's Register of Corporations Directors and Executives will also provide what you need. Many industry and business journals have annual issues that list the top 500 companies in their field. Fortune Magazine is one, and Adweek is another. These can be obtained in reference libraries or at the newsstands.

Subscribe to trade publications in your specialty. They usually list announcements of executive position changes. You may spot the name of someone you have been calling on who has moved on to another company. You may find that a new person has been hired to replace the person you were calling on. In addition, any new persons appointed to the departments you usually work with are prospects for business. New people on the job may be looking to establish their own sources for graphic design, photography and illustration.

These publications also usually carry announcements of new business start-ups. This is a good source of leads for companies that may be prospects for logo designs, business letterheads, identity programs, and promotion print assignments.

Composing a Sales Letter

Writing a sales letter is not much different from writing an ad. The form differs but the approach is basically the same.

Start off with an idea that will get their attention. Think in terms of the benefits to the reader, rather than what it is you do. The old selling cliche, "sell the sizzle, not the steak" still makes good sense.

You may want to write a clever letter, or a humorous letter, or a straight on-target no non-sense letter. The letter can reflect your own advertising or selling philosophy. In fact, try them all! Find the one that works for you. In any case, your letter should contain these essentials:

A description of your services, and an indication of why they are important to the reader.

If appropriate, tell about your success in working with companies in the same field as the prospect.

If possible, tell about your facilities, ability to meet tough deadlines, and your competitive pricing.

Ask for the order, suggest that they call you, or that you will call them to set up a meeting. Or enclose a self-addressed stamped postcard that they can fill in and return requesting a meeting.

Keep a record of which letters were sent to which prospects. Each letter should be followed-up with a phone call within a few days of their receipt of your letter. Seven or ten days later they may not remember the letter.

SAMPLE LETTER #1

Mr. A. Smith, President
The XYZ Freight Company
1234 Main Street
Oblivion, N.J.

Mr. Smith;

Will you be ready for the tough selling days that are ahead? If your plans include developing sales brochures, you will want to know how the Bukar Co. can help.

We can create an entire promotion program or work with you on any part you need.

We know the freight business. We've worked with some of the leading companies in your field:

The DDD Company

GHI Hauling Co.

JKL Express Inc.

We have been successful because we can be depended upon:

* to produce a creative product at a competitive price

* to meet your tightest deadline

I will call to arrange to meet with you, so that we can discuss how we may work with you on your next promotion.

Sincerely,

SAMPLE LETTER #2

Mr E. Entrepreneur
The new company
12-34 Wide Boulevard
Market City, New York

Mr. Entrepreneur;

Start your company off with the right image. A new company can quickly gain high visibility in its field by the excellence of its products and services and the skillful use of graphic communication skills.

Graphic image building, the consistent use of a group of representative images can be created to symbolize your company where it interacts with its market.

I can provide you with a number of interesting case histories of successful programs we have created for a number of leading companies.

Let us meet and discuss your needs without any obligation on your part.

Have your secretary call 1-800-000 0000 to arrange a meeting at a mutually convenient time.

Cordially,

SAMPLE LETTER #3

Mr. J. Jones
The First Public Corporation
Bond Street
Finance City, CA

Mr. Jones;

It's almost Annual Report time again. Are you tired of doing the same old thing year after year?

It may be time for a new approach.

Consider the Bukar Studio. We have been designing award-winning annual reports for companies just like yours.

We can take complete responsibility, from concept, through production and printing. And you may be amazed at how far even a small budget can go towards producing a professional report with fresh image-building appeal.

Let me show you what we have done for others and if you are interested, what we can do for you.

There is no obligation. Let's set up a meeting.

Cordially,

6

Turning Prospects into Clients/ Selling Yourself

Selling yourself is nothing more than convincing the prospective client/buyer that your particular talent is what he needs; that you can do the work at a competitive price; and that you work in a professional, business-like manner.

Our personality, our sample portfolio, how we dress, speak, act, what we do, say, what we don't say all contribute to what we communicate to the client/buyer at that crucial first meeting.

Art buyers meeting an unfamiliar artist, even one with great samples will need a lot of convincing before they will take a chance on using the artist. If they give out an assignment, and it isn't done right, their job could be on the line. The artist must in this first meeting inspire the level of confidence needed to be trusted with an assignment. This level of confidence is a result of how you handle yourself during this important first session and the subsequent methods you use to follow up.

WHAT TO SAY AND WHAT NOT TO SAY

If you're inexperienced, it's not to your benefit to tell how long you are in the business. If you are experienced it will be evident and the subject will not come up. In this business it's not advantageous to be either young and inexperienced, or old with too many years of experience.

When you enter an office and start to set-up your

presentation, be prepared with a short introductory statement that can hold the buyer's interest while you're preparing your materials. Start with the broad picture; who you are and what you do. For example:

> *"Hello Mr. Smith, I'm Jack Spratt. I'm here to show you some interesting annual reports I have designed and produced for companies similar to yours. May I set up here on this desk?"*

As you show each sample, tell something about it that will explain why you did it the way that you did. If you can, tell about the positive results from its use. "Sales went up 3%" or "The board of directors was really pleased."

Be prepared to tell, if asked, what your charges were for the work you're showing. Also the prospect may want to know how much time it took to produce. If you produced the sample in an impressively short time, tell about it as part of its story. Buyers want to know that you have the ability and knowledge to get things done when time is exceptionally short.

Limit your presentation of samples to approximately 10-15 minutes. Do it at a comfortable pace. Don't rush through it. Practice it so that it fits smoothly into that time slot. You want to leave some time at the end. The buyer may want to ask you some questions about your company, or make some comments about your work. When the meeting is over remember to hand the buyer your business card, and any promotional materials you have for his file before you leave.

Be prepared. Develop answers to all the questions you can think of. You may be asked about your background, or your experience, other design specialties or why you picked a particular color or format for a sample you are showing.

Later, consider any important comments that were made. These comments can provide valuable insights into the samples that you have chosen and into the personality of the buyer.

It is very important to speak with confidence, with assurance, if you want the buyer to believe in your ability to do a job for him. He can't believe in you, if you appear to be uncomfortable and unsure of yourself. It's not unusual to feel a little uneasy when you first start out, but that will disappear as your confidence grows. One of the best ways to build confidence, is to rehearse your presentation. Practice it over and over again until you know it thoroughly. Role playing with another person can be very valuable, or just go over imaginary situations in your head, making the points that you would make as if you were in a client's office. Either method will soon have you making a smooth presentation.

> *As an art director I had to present the ads for a new campaign at client meetings and at new business presentations. These situations are always nerve-wracking since so much is at stake. Most of my presentations went smoothly. This surprised my co-workers because they never saw me rehearse. What they didn't know was that I used the hour ride into the office on the railroad to sit quietly and prepare what I was going to say.*

71

I would go over the ads visualizing the situation in my imagination. Once I decided what I was going to say I repeated the presentation from beginning to end as many times as I could. When my train arrived in New York I was ready.

PUTTING YOUR BEST FOOT FORWARD

First and foremost;

Keep appointments and be on time. If you must cancel or change an appointment, give the buyer as much advance notice as possible.

Dress properly for a new business presentation. Use your own common sense. The basics are;

- o Look clean and neat, hair combed, shoes shined, face cleanly shaved.

- o Mustache or beard neatly trimmed.

Clothing styles and dress codes are fluid; they change with the times. Creative people have always dressed in the most up-to-date styles. I would advise that you dress business-like, and accessorize with something up to the minute to bring forth your individuality.

KNOW YOUR PROSPECT

Learn everything you can about a prospect before you call on him. If you know what kind of things he likes or dislikes, you can tailor your presentation to make the best impression. If someone has suggested that you call on this person, don't be shy, ask the person to tell you what they know about the prospect. The prospects, themselves, will give you a lot of information, if you keep your eyes and ears open. There's information in the room when you meet them. What is on the walls? Is their desk neat, well organized, or messy, with piles of papers everywhere?

You are calling on this person because you have been led to believe that he is the purchaser. His title may lead you to believe that he is, but in fact he may not be the person that you really need to see. Tune in to what is going on in his office. A chance phone conversation that interrupts your presentation may give you some insight into the situation. A person that steps into the room and asks a question may inadvertently provide you with the answer. This is not an uncommon problem. Some buyers designate their assistants as the person to see. This helps them not waste time seeing every unknown artist that calls.

Learn to read body language. There are a number of good books on the subject. You will be able to tell if the prospect is interested, or bored. Are they reacting positively to you or are you turning them off? Learn to interpret the information you are getting.

Alter your presentation accordingly. Don't rigidly make your presentation the same way each time you give it. Spend more time where the prospect seems interested; skip over parts you don't think he wants to see.

As you will quickly learn, not all client/buyers are courteous, patient or even nice people. Like any group they come in all varieties of personality. You may have rushed to get to their office on time, only to find yourself seated in their waiting room for 45 minutes. How you respond to that kind of treatment is up to you. When it happens I would say that most of the time it was probably unavoidable. What the buyer says when he finally comes out to get you is the clue. If they offer an apology or a reasonable explanation, it's acceptable. It happens to all of us once in a while. But if there is no explanation and it is completely ignored, then the person may be someone you would not want to do business with in the future.

THE TEST ASSIGNMENT

You have made all the right moves, said all the right things, and this prospect calls you with an assignment. It's possible that you called just at the right time. There is an assignment on his desk that needs to be done immediately, and he thinks you're perfect for this job. And even more important he has time enough to give it to someone else if you don't come through. He has an opportunity to see what you can do, without getting himself into hot water. He's not doing you a favor, good sources are important to him. Here is the opportunity you have been waiting for. Satisfy him now and you assuredly will continue to get business from him in the future.

Be businesslike. Don't waste time with idle

chatter beyond what is necessary to establish rapport.

Make sure you get all the information you need to do the assignment. Ask about purpose, style, colors, quantity, size, delivery date, and get agreement on the price. ASK FOR A PURCHASE ORDER!!! When you have what you need, leave.

Deliver the job on time, preferably in person. Go over it with the client. If there are corrections to be done, and you can't convince him that they aren't necessary, don't complain, or beat it into the ground. Unless the changes are unreasonable, and require that much of the job be done over; be gracious, do them quickly, give him what he wants.

Disagreements over esthetics are common. Be a person who is easy to deal with. Find the magic line between being reasonable, and compromising your design principles to the vanishing point. Defend your ideas if the client seems to be willing to listen. But don't be a prima dona, certainly not on the first assignment. Experience will tell you how far you should go. Discuss difficult situations with your friends in the business. See if they would have handled the problem any differently.

You have delivered your first job to this particular client. Now, before you leave it's a good idea to inquire if there are any other assignments coming up that you could do for them. If they're happy, you may walk out with another assignment.

When the assignment is completed, delivered and accepted, bill it immediately. Sending invoices weeks after the work was done is begging for problems. The client may not remember that it was a rush job that required late night hours, or they may get it mixed up with another job that went bad. Bill it while it's fresh in their mind, and avoid problems.

Remember that a client's perception of you consists of a lot more than the work you deliver. Your value as an artist is of little interest if you can not provide the services that are required. Delivering a job late leaves a bad impression even if the job is great. Being argumentative, or always complaining about price, or problems with the job marks you as an unpleasant person to deal with. Besides delivering good work, you have to be conscious of the clients needs and provide appropriate services to make life easier for the client. Being someone who understands, and can be depended upon is the answer to every client's prayers.

Clients can be unfair and unreasonable. Typically they are selfishly concerned with their own deadlines and don't care about your problems. You may over a period of time turn out ten terrific jobs for a client, and lose them when you have to turn them down because you are already overloaded beyond your production capabilities.

Nobody wants to lose a good account. Here is how to approach this situation:

Attempt to extend the time available to

> produce the work.   Do not assume that
> the deadline is an absolute unchangeable
> circumstance.   In many cases clients ask
> for work days before they really need it.
> They want to protect themselves by al-
> lowing time for changes, or any unforseen
> circumstance that may occur. If the client
> knows that you may have to refuse the
> assignment and he has additional time he
> probably will extend the deadline.

It is negotiable. You ask for three more days. The
client says impossible, but they can give you till
noon the next day. You reply you need a minimum of two more days to produce the job right.
You both compromise. You get more time to do
the job. Now you can fit it into your busy
schedule. The client still gets the work when he
really need it.

If the deadline is real and an extension isn't
negotiable, before turning it down, and jeopard-
izing the relationship, consider this other possibility:

> Sub-contract the work out to a free-lancer.
> It's more expensive this way. You may
> even end up not making anything on the
> job. If the account is a good one that you
> want to keep happy this still makes sense,
> if the alternative is losing the account's
> business.

Negotiating delivery deadlines is not only for
emergency situations. You will be surprised
how many pressure situations can be relieved by
getting a few more days or a few additional
hours for an assignment.

77

CHAPTER

7

Record Keeping/
Files
and Forms

Record keeping is a nuisance at best. Particularly for creative people. Nevertheless it is important to the successful functioning of any business.

As you operate your business you will find that questions keep coming up, and you need to have the answers right at your fingertips. A client wants to know why the latest job you're doing is more than the last job.

A client wants to question an item on the estimate you submitted 4 weeks ago. The tax people want to know how much you made last year. You want to know if you're making any money. You want to know which jobs are profitable and which jobs are not.

These are just a few of the many questions that keep coming up when you operate a business.

Set up a system of files that you are comfortable with but keep them up to date. Otherwise they will be useless. Experience will tell you what you need, but here is a basic list of the three major record categories that should get you started.

Set up files that will provide you with information on;

1. Work in Process

2. Work recently completed

3. Work completed 6 months, a year or more before

1. Work in Process.

You will first of all need a record of every job you do. This record should contain all the information on that job.

Some artists and agencies use a large envelope, with a printed form on the outside for entering the information about the job. The envelope will hold all the supplier invoices for that job until the job is billed.

Others prefer using a three ring notebook filled with pre-printed job sheet forms.

The information that you need to record on the job sheet, or envelope is:

On the front side:
- ❏ Job Number
- ❏ Date Received
- ❏ Clients Purchase Order Number
- ❏ Client Name (person to contact)
- ❏ Job Description;
    (Specifications)
- ❏ Delivery Date
- ❏ Estimated Cost Quoted to Client
- ❏ Date of Invoice
- ❏ Amount of Invoice

On the other side of the Job Sheet are categories used to record both estimated costs, and the actual costs to produce the job:

	ESTIMATED COST	ACTUAL COST
Layout	_____	_____
Illustration	_____	_____
Mechanicals	_____	_____
Type Spec.	_____	_____
Type Setting	_____	_____
Photography	_____	_____
Photostats	_____	_____
Retouching	_____	_____
Misc.	_____	_____
_____	_____	_____
_____	_____	_____
_____	_____	_____
_____	_____	_____
Color Separations	_____	_____
Printing	_____	_____

TOTAL COST _____   SELLING PRICE _____

Mark-up _____   Sales Tax _____

TOTAL _____   TOTAL _____

If you are using a job envelope, all the information should be on only one side of the sheet.

If a job envelope is used, store all the important papers pertaining to that job in the envelope, such as purchase order, bills from suppliers, time records, copies of your estimate. Otherwise you will need to store them in separate files.

When the job is completed, enter the costs from all the invoices and time sheets in the envelope, onto the outside job sheet for easy reference when making-up your invoice. ·

After entering all the amounts, and the invoice has been written, the supplier invoices should be removed and filed in a folder marked "BILLS TO BE PAID".

As you pay these bills they are transferred to another file folder headed "PAID BILLS-19__"(YEAR)

A copy of your invoice for the job should be filed under "CURRENT INVOICES-Unpaid". When the invoice is paid it is moved to another file folder marked 'CURRENT INVOICES-Paid".

If you do not choose to use the envelope with form method, use a one or two sided form, as outlined above. The forms can have three holes punched and stored in a ring binder. They can be grouped by sections for each client or by consecutive job numbers, or any other grouping that makes sense to you.

Every job should be assigned a job number when it is started, and the job sheet filled out.

Some companies use a combination of letters and

numbers to identify each job. The letters can represent the initials of the client. One way of zeroing in on a particular client's job.

For example:

> The client's name is ALBA GEARS, all the job numbers would start with AG,
>
> > AG10
> >
> > AG11
> >
> > AG12, etc.
>
> Another clients name is GOLD SERV-ICES, the numbers would all start with GS,
>
> > GS10
> >
> > GS11, etc.

2) Work in the recent past

As you have already seen, you need to set up a file to keep continuing records readily at hand.

You could start with a small letter size table top file box. If you are successful you will probably need at least a two drawer letter size file very soon.

I recommend that you use the hanging folders rather than the standard manila folders. The identification tabs on these folders can be changed and the folders re-used for many years.

So far we have talked about having files for incoming supplier invoices, both paid and unpaid, and files for your outgoing invoices, paid and unpaid. You will also need files for;

- ☐ ESTIMATES
- ☐ PROPOSALS
- ☐ TAX FORMS
- ☐ BANK STATEMENTS
- ☐ SALES LETTERS
- ☐ PUBLICITY & PROMOTION
- ☐ PURCHASE ORDERS

3. Work completed 6 months, a year, or earlier

As your business progresses, and your files start to fill up, you will want to transfer jobs that are at least six months old to another section of your file cabinet. This will make it easier to work with the current files. After some time you may want to free up more space in your file cabinets. Remove the files which are more than a year old to either another file cabinet kept for that purpose, or cardboard transfer file boxes for placement in a storage area.

BASIC BOOKKEEPING

In addition you will need to set up some system of bookkeeping to record: sales, cash receipts, and cash disbursements.

The sales record is a listing of each invoice that you send out. Combined with the cash receipts record it provides you with a running monthly record of how much was billed out, and which invoices have been paid or have not been paid.

The cash dispersements record lists every purchase you make — from petty cash to buying printing. It provides you with a cumulative monthly record of how much you are spending in each category listed.

A) Setting up a Sales/Cash Receipts Record

If you are a computer person and have a PC you will want to keep your bookkeeping records stored or backed up on floppy discs. Purchase spreadsheet software, and use the program with the information that follows to create your sales, cash receipts and cash disbursements records. If you are not going to use a computer, the simplest system you can start requires nothing more than a lined notebook, the kind used in elementary school. Or you can purchase standard ledger paper and a post binder at your local stationery store. Ledger papers come in a variety of column configurations. Decide how many columns you have to set up before you make your purchase.

The basic SALES record should have the following headings for vertical columns going across the top of the page:

Invoice Date	Client	Amount Billed	Sales Tax	

also continuing across the top:

Total Billed	Date Paid	Amount Paid	

You can add additional columns for partial payments, and dates of partial payments if you are going to do large projects that require partial payments as the job progresses.

If you have many entries each month it would be a good idea to have a separate page for each month. Leave space at the bottom of each month/ page for the totaling of each column.

At the end of the year set up a page with the same columns and enter each months total figures. Totaling the columns will give you your complete yearly sales figures.

	Sales	Sales Tax	Total Amount
January	2500.	206.25	2706.25
February	5970.	492.52	6462.52
March	4750.	391.88	5141.88

B) Setting up a Cash Disbursements Record

You will want to pay your bills with checks. You probably have a personal checking account now, but it's advisable to open up another account so that your personal funds and the business funds don't intermingle. If you intermingle your funds, you will never really know how you are doing, and your records will end up a mess. There may be legal requirements that mandate that you keep separate accounts. If you have business expenses that are tax deductible, they can be disallowed if mixed with your personal expenses.

In a notebook or ledger, set up the following vertical columns:

|DATE | CHECK TO | CK# | AMOUNT | GENERAL |

Continue with the following additional columns for services you will be regularly purchasing like;

|TYPE | PRINTING | PHOTOGRAPHY |FREELANCERS|

Here you will enter every check paid out during each month. Leave a few empty spaces at the bottom of each month for the totals of each column.

> You enter the date of the check first,
> to whom the check was paid,
> the check number in the next column.
> The amount of the check in the next column.

> Then enter the amount of the check <u>again</u>, under the column that best describes the product or services purchased. Typesetting, Photography, Printing, Etc.

Naturally you will establish those categories that are pertinent to your own business.

The checks that are issued for other products or services that do not fit in any other category are entered in the general column. That would include monthly checks made for petty cash; rent; telephone and lease or purchase of equipment. Other expenditures like transportation, entertainment, postage, legal and accounting fees would also be listed under the general column.

At the end of the year, make up a page listing the

monthly totals in the same way that you obtained the yearly figures for cash receipts. At the end of the year you will know at a glance how much you spent for printing, typesetting, etc.

Remember you may be required to justify any expenses you have incurred while conducting your business. Ask for taxi and bridge toll receipts. Get receipts for everything and keep a careful calender notebook of all meetings, travel expenses, entertainment, etc.

You have here a minimum bookkeeping setup. It will do to get you started. It would be a good idea to check your system out with an accountant or bookkeeper you know. In any case it is a good idea, to establish a relationship with an accountant. You will probably need help when it's time to file tax returns.

As you continue in business you will find that you need to create many additional files. If your records are well organized you will avoid frequent, frantic, time-wasting searches for missing information, and you will have more time for the creative aspects of running your business.

8

Doing Business on Credit

Unlike consumers who make their purchases either by paying cash or with credit cards, most business is conducted on a credit basis.

In business, buying on credit is certainly more convenient. Imagine if you had to keep a large amount of money on hand at all times to pay for photography, or for a typesetting job. You would be running back and forth to the bank everyday. And think of the security problem having cash around at all times.

If you are contemplating going into business in the near future, or thinking of making a major purchase, like a home, do something about establishing a good credit rating now. If not, you may find it difficult to obtain credit of any kind when you need it.

You can do this by borrowing a small amount of money from your bank, and paying it back in regular payments. Borrow the money even if you don't need the money. It will establish a favorable credit record for your future use.

But buying what you need on credit doesn't just happen. You can't say ok I will do business on credit and it will magically happen.

You have to establish credit with those suppliers you will be making purchases from on a regular basis. Actually it is surprisingly easy to do.

BUYING ON CREDIT

Most graphic art suppliers, typesetters, art materials suppliers, and free-lancers will readily extend credit to you. They will ask that you fill out a credit information form. The credit application will require certain basic information about your company.

Questions like these:

> How long are you in business?

> At what bank is the company account?

> The names of companies that you are doing business with on credit? The amount of business (dollars) you expect to do with the company?

If you are starting out and have no credit references as yet, one way to get started and work your way into a credit relationship is to pay for your first few orders on a C.O.D (cash) basis. Then after a few transactions tell the suppler that you would like to continue purchasing from them, on a credit basis. Most suppliers will readily agree.

Use your personal credit references if you have nothing else. If you have bought a house or furniture on time and have made regular payments, or use a credit card and are not behind in your payments, give those company names as reference. Use the names of friends in the business (with their permission) as personal references.

Once you have established credit with one company use it as a reference to establish other credit relationships.

When you have established credit with your suppliers, you will want to pay their invoices on time, and keep your credit rating in good standing.

They will indicate on their invoices their credit terms. Under TERMS it will say something like "net 10 days". This indicates that they request full payment within ten days of their invoice date.

It may say "2 percent 10 days/net 30 days", which means you can deduct 2% if you pay within 10 days. Or you can pay the full amount if you wait for 30 days.

If you are going to use freelancers to help out at busy periods, it's a good idea to pay them at the end of the week, if you can do it, rather than at the end of the month. You will find it easier to get help when you need it. Freelancers will give you preference over other companies that pay monthly.

SELLING ON CREDIT

Business runs on credit. You buy on credit, and you have to sell on credit.

If your clients are large national companies, you are not likely to have much trouble, at least not with their obligations to their suppliers. Nevertheless it is important to understand that non-payment difficulties do occur. However, there are ways both to prevent their occurrence and to deal with them when they do happen.

Your first line of defense is the Purchase Order.

Always, and I can't emphasize this enough, <u>always</u> get a signed purchase order when you accept an assignment.

Most companies, both large and small, issue purchase orders. It's a basic part of any accounting system. Companies use purchase orders to keep control of their purchases.

If there ever is a question about collecting for an assignment, the purchase order is proof hard to refute, either in a discussion, or in a court of law.

The purchase order, to have full value as a contract, should contain:

- ❑   The P.O. number
- ❑   The date P.O. is issued
- ❑   The name of the company to whom it is issued
- ❑   A description of the work to be done
- ❑   The price
- ❑   The delivery date
- ❑   Signature of the buyer

The P.O. should also contain a statement as to the terms of the sale. Is the work being sold with one time reproduction rights only, or is the work being sold outright. What rights does the artist retain?

If you're dealing with a small company for the first time, and it's going to be a large job involving more time and money than you can afford to get stuck for, get credit references. If it's a small job, trust your gut feelings, give them the benefit of any doubts, AND GET A PURCHASE OR-DER.

What kind of credit references should you ask for?

1. The name of their bank. Call their bank and ask for the amount of their balance. You will not be told the actual amount, but you will be told that it is in the upper five figures (75,000 to 99,000) or low six figures, (100,000 to 400,000). That will give you an idea of their size and financial strength.

2. The names of two or three companies they purchase from. Call the companies. Inquire as to how promptly they pay their bills. Ask for the approximate amount of credit they have extend to that company.

If for some reason you are uncomfortable with what you hear and want to check further, call the local Better Business Bureau, and/or the local office of the Department of Labor. If either one has a file on them, examine the reports carefully before making a decision.

You do not have to turn the job down if the report raises questions about extending credit to the company. Break the job down into stages, so much for research and development, so much for layouts and copy, so much for production, and so much for printing. Request that payment of the first phase be made up front, before you start work. Propose payment of each additional phase upon delivery or approval. If they accept, make sure you are NOT PRESSURED BY DEADLINES, TO PROCEED TO THE NEXT PHASE BEFORE YOU HAVE PAYMENT FOR THE LAST PHASE. IF PAYMENT IS NOT FORTHCOMING DO NOT PROCEED WITH THE JOB. If they are not conforming to the agreed upon procedure you are not obligated to continue. Following this routine will limit any possible losses to only one phase at a time. IF YOU ALLOW YOURSELF TO BE PUSHED INTO CONTINUING WORK WITHOUT PAYMENT, YOU OPEN YOURSELF UP TO GREATER LOSSES.

If you do not get a good credit report on a company, walk away. Don't work with them, no matter how hungry you may be for the work. You will probably have trouble collecting. You will have to fight for your money. You will have to argue about the agreed upon charges. You will have to wait a long time for your payments. Use the time instead to find a better new account. Don't waste it on companies just looking for a sucker to stick.

PROTECT YOURSELF

Here is a common ploy used by small businesses when negotiating a project with a designer. It's a good idea to listen, be sympathetic, but don't fall for it.

They will tell you their plans for doing great things later on, which they will be happy to assign to you, if you would only cooperate and do this job for a special low price. It's the old donkey going for the carrot on the stick. The donkey never can reach the carrot, and neither will you ever make it up on that promised big job, because there isn't any. You will find that this kind of client will bargain you down, and cry poverty on every job. When you refuse to do it after the first few jobs he will leave you to find another sucker to extend the carrot to.

Protect yourself. Always quote a price you can live with. That means a price that provides you with a profit. If it's a minimum profit, it's OK. <u>But don't work for nothing on any job!!</u>

As smart as you are, as hard as you try to protect yourself, someone, somewhere, sometime, somehow will not pay an invoice, and no matter what you do you will not be able to collect. It is a fact of life in the business world. All you can do is minimize the possibility of losses, by keeping a tight reign on your credit controls.

Protection means get it in writing. Do not depend on verbal understandings. That doesn't mean that every job requires a lawyer and a contract be drawn up. Get a purchase order or write a letter of understanding, spelling out everything that has been agreed upon; start and completion dates; method of payment; describe the work to be done; the quantities to be delivered; and any other pertinent details that have been agreed upon. Send two copies to your client, sign both copies and indicate a space for your client to sign one and date it. He should sign one copy and return it to you. That way you both have signed copies of the agreement.

This will eliminate most of the arguments that occur after a job is completed over what was or wasn't supposed to be done.

If a client agrees to a proposal for approval and payment of a job at each stage of production, and explains in the middle of the job that they are having a short term cash flow problem, and they can't pay for this phase, you have a tough choice to make. If you refuse to continue without payment, the client will point out the importance of having the job by the agreed upon date, and that the job is of little use if delivered after that date.

What do you do?

If you proceed with the work you are putting yourself in jeopardy. You don't really know the condition of the company. They may be in very bad shape, even on the verge of bankruptcy. If that turns out to be the case you will never be paid. If they really are tight for money it means that you may have to wait for your money for quite some time. What about your suppliers, will they wait for payment?

DON'T GO AHEAD WITHOUT SOME PAYMENT, UNLESS: THE CLIENT AGREES TO AND MEETS A PAYMENT DATE FOR THE UNPAID BALANCE THAT IS WELL BEFORE THE FINAL DELIVERY DATE, AND AGREES TO PAY THE BALANCE DUE UPON DELIVERY OF THE JOB. AND GET THE AGREEMENT IN WRITING!

An additional safeguard would be to have the client sign a personal promissory note or several notes that total the amount owed. The notes become due upon agreed upon dates and spread the payments out over an agreed upon period of time. Because they are personal notes they are secured by personal assets, like a house, a car, or a boat. If the client does not make payment of a note on the date required, you can proceed through the courts to obtain his assets in lieu of payment.

Promissory notes are a standard form that can be obtained in any good stationery store.

Be especially wary of new small businesses just starting up. While most are honest in their dealings, there are a few bad apples worth watching out for.

They generally come to a designer with nice projects — they need stationery, logo designs, promotion literature, advertising, a lot of work, it looks inviting. It looks like a good account.

The problem is that if the business succeeds everyone gets paid; if it doesn't, the suppliers take the loss and not the client. When you try to collect, you may find that the corporation has no assets, or they're in another state, or some other legal complication that makes collecting impossible. To your dismay, you discover that it is you who have unwittingly financed this losing business and not the client.

The answer is, get some cash up-front and the balance upon delivery for every job you do for a new company. And <u>do not deliver</u> unless you receive payment!

9

Collecting Overdue Invoices

It can be maddening. You've worked hard to get the business. You've worked late and over weekends to meet your client's deadlines. You've sent your invoice, and here it is four months later and you still haven't been paid.

It's not fair. It's not the way it should be. But that's what happens time and time again. It's a fact of business life. I said it before, no matter how smart you are, no matter how careful you are, if you stay in business long enough someone is going to stick you with an unpaid invoice.

We have already touched on some of the things that you can do to minimize your exposure to this kind of situation. Now let's talk about keeping a late payment from turning into a bad debt.

Most companies that take more than 30 days to pay their supplier invoices aren't thieves. They may be a small company that is having a cash flow problem. They need to receive payment from their customers to be able to pay your bill. Sometimes it's company policy. When interest rates are high, and borrowing is expensive, companies pay slowly holding on to their cash as long as possible. Payment in 90 to 120 days is not uncommon. Smaller companies run into slow business periods, use up their cash reserves and they can't pay their bills until things get better.

This doesn't mean that you have to accept the situation. You don't care about their problems. You need the money now, not in three or four more months.

First Rule:

Never lose track of unpaid invoices. Set up a control system. You have to know how long each bill is out there.

Let's say that 30 days plus or minus a few days is a reasonable time within which you would expect to get paid. When an invoice pops up on your list that is 30 days old and unpaid, you must not wait, you must call immediately to find out why it has not been paid. If there is a problem straighten it out. If there is no problem find out when it will be paid. The answer will probably be something like "We'll pay it soon", or some other unspecific, indefinite answer.

Second Rule:

Never, never accept an indefinite answer. You must get them to commit to a specific date.

You ask:	*"Can I expect a check on Friday?"*
Client:	*"No, maybe the week after."*
You answer:	*"Can I expect the check then on Wednesday of that week?"*
Client:	*"O.K., I will try and get you the check by Wednesday."*

Third Rule:

Follow up on the client's commitment. You must be tenacious.

If Wednesday comes around and there is no check, you must immediately call the client again.

You call:	*"Mr. Smith, it's Wednesday and I have not received the check you promised to send me."*
Client:	*"I mailed it out yesterday, you probably will get it in tomorrow's mail."*

The client, if left to his own devices, will stall for as long as you allow him to get away with it.

During this period of stalling, you don't know whether the client intends to pay you eventually or never to pay you at all. That is what you have to determine.

Insisting on a commitment places the client in the position that he has to pay to keep his word. If he does not pay, he either exposes himself as a deadbeat, or reveals that his business is in trouble. In either case knowing sooner rather than later can help you save the situation.

You can collect from a business that is in trouble. But within a few months, it can turn into a bankrupt situation and then you probably will not collect anything.

Let's assume that you received a commitment to be paid by a certain day. That day comes and there is no check. Now, you must confront the client on not coming through with his promise to pay.

When that happens you have to use every means

at your disposal to get as much money out of the client in the shortest time possible. Depending on what the client's excuses are, you probably have a business in bad trouble, or a dishonest client. Ask for immediate payment. Offer to send a messenger to pick up the check. The client will probably again offer to pay some time in the future. Again insist on a precise commitment but, only within the next few days. If they do not deliver on that commitment, call again, be angry, tell them you want to come over and pick up the check right now.

During this phase you will begin having difficulty getting the client on the phone. Use any means you can devise to get through to your client. One devise that works is to give the operator another name, and then identify yourself when she puts you through.

You now have a real collection problem. If the debt is four months old, and the client is not meeting his promised payments, start thinking about possible legal action.

It's time for your final effort to get payment. Ask for a partial payment, get him to agree to a payment schedule that you can both live with. A check every week, or every month until it's all paid up. But only on the condition that the first payment be made right now. Get it in writing. Or, have the client sign a series of promissory notes, one for each payment. As he makes the payments the notes are returned.

Getting some of the money is better than getting none at all. If you can collect this way, I think it's preferable to going to court.

Keep the pressure on the client to commit to a date and to honor his commitment. When the client can't pay all his debts, you bet he is going to pay the one that keeps bothering him the most.

If none of these efforts have produced payment, it's time to send a letter relating the facts; that you have been unable to reach him; that he has not met his promised commitments, and that you will start a suit to collect if you do not receive a check by such and such a date.

If they do not respond with a check, or a specific date for settlement, you should file a claim in Small Claims Court. If the amount you want to recover is too large for that court, consult a lawyer or collection agency.

If you keep on your toes, and follow the procedures outlined here you have a good chance of keeping most slow payment situations from turning into non-paying situations.

Conclusion

If you have read this far you should now have a good understanding of what to realistically expect. Adapt and use the information you have learned. It will help to conduct you more safely through the maze of business shenanigans that await the artist adventuring into this new territory.

Some of the things suggested to be done for self protection are not easy to do. It's hard to turn down work when you need it badly. It's not easy to be hard-nosed about up-front payments from new clients you are afraid of offending. You may feel it's demeaning to go after overdue payments. As difficult as you may find these things to do, you must be tough. Prevention, that is, not allowing the predators to place you in a vulnerable position is the only protection you have.

You will find to your surprise that the legitimate clients you deal with will rarely object to the working terms suggested here. To them, they're nothing new. It is the way business is done. It is precisely those clients that do object that you have to be wary of.

There are artists who think about going on their own and reject the idea, believing that they have to be a star designer to succeed out there. You don't. There is room for everyone. No matter what your ability as a designer, there's a client waiting for you. Looking for just your kind of product.

Reach for the top, confident in the knowledge

that if you fall a little short, there's still plenty of opportunity to go around.

I wish you all success in your business, and hope that I have been able to save you from experiencing some of the bumps and bruises I had to endure.

Standard Directory of Advertisers is published by National Register Publishing Company. Macmillan Directory Div.

Standard & Poor's Register of Corporations, Directors and Executives is published by Standard & Poor's Corporation.

Adweek is published by A/S/M Communications, Inc.

Fortune Magazine is published by the Time Magazine Co.

Xerox is a registered trademark of Xerox Corporation.

About the Author

After gaining experience working for a number of advertising agencies and art studios and then freelancing for some years as an art director and graphic designer, Nat Bukar spent the next 20 years as a partner in an art studio, a sales promotion agency, and an advertising agency. There were good years and there were not so good years. He learned what worked by doing lots of things that didn't work. In the process he learned how to operate a design business in the toughest marketplace in the country: New York City.